Gibbons
v. Ogden
Controlling Trade
Between States

Isabel Simone Levinson

Landmark Supreme Court Cases

Enslow Publishers, Inc.

44 Fadem Road   PO Box 38
Box 699   Aldershot
Springfield, NJ 07081   Hants GU12 6BP
USA   UK

http://www.enslow.com

Library of Congress Cataloging-in-Publication Data

Levinson, Isabel Simone.
    Gibbons v. Ogden: controlling trade between states / Isabel Simone Levinson.
        p. cm. — (Landmark Supreme Court cases)
    Includes bibliographical references and index.
    Summary: Describes the Supreme Court case concerning the steamboat monopoly
between New York state and New Jersey, which established the right of Congress to
regulate interstate commerce.
    ISBN 0-7660-1086-4
    1. Gibbons, Thomas, 1757–1826—Trials, litigation, etc.—Juvenile literature.
2. Ogden, Aaron, 1756–1839—Trials, litigation, etc.—Juvenile literature. 3. Livingston, Robert R.,
1746–1813—Trials, litigation, etc.—Juvenile literature. 4. Fulton, Robert, 1765–1815—Trials,
litigation, etc.—Juvenile literature. 5. Interstate commerce—Law and legislation—United States—
Juvenile literature. 6. Constitutional history—United States—Juvenile literature. 7. Inland
navigation—Law and legislation—United States—Juvenile literature. [1. Gibbons, Thomas,
1757–1826—Trials, litigation, etc. 2. Ogden, Aaron, 1756–1839—Trials, litigation, etc.
3. Interstate commerce. 4. United States Supreme Court.] II. Title: Gibbons versus Ogden.
III. Series.
    KF228.G53L48 1999
    343.73'088—DC21   98-34011
                                                        CIP
                                                         AC

Printed in the United States of America

10 9 8 7 6 5 4 3 2 1

To Our Readers:
All Internet addresses in this book were active and appropriate when we went to press. Any comments or
suggestions can be sent by e-mail to Comments@enslow.com or to the address on the back cover.

Photo Credits: Courtesy Library of Congress, pp. 83, 89, 93; Courtesy New-York Historical Society,
Reproduced from the *Dictionary of American Portraits* published by Dover Publications, Inc., 1967, pp. 51,
82; Courtesy New York Public Library, p. 11; Dane Peland photographer, "Collection of the Supreme Court
of the United States," p. 97; Engraving by Albert Rosenthal from a painting by John Wesley Jarvis,
Reproduced from the *Dictionary of American Portraits* published by Dover Publications, Inc., 1967, p. 66;
Engraving by Alexander H. Richie, Reproduced from the *Dictionary of American Portraits* published by
Dover Publications, Inc., 1967, p. 40; Engraving by J. Cheney after a drawing by William Wetmore Story,
Reproduced from the *Dictionary of American Portraits* published by Dover Publications, Inc., 1967, p. 59;
Engraving by John W. Orr, Reproduced from the *Dictionary of American Portraits* published by Dover
Publications, Inc., 1967, p. 34; Franz Jantzen, "Collection of the Supreme Court of the United States," p. 57;
Painting attributed to James Sharples, Sr., Courtesy Independence National Historical Park, Reproduced
from the *Dictionary of American Portraits* published by Dover Publications, Inc., 1967, p. 68; Painting by
Charles William Peale, Courtesy Independence National Historical Park, Reproduced from the *Dictionary of
American Portraits* published by Dover Publications, Inc., 1967, p. 9; Painting by Gilbert Stuart, Reproduced
from the *Dictionary of American Portraits* published by Dover Publications, Inc., 1967, p. 7; Painting by
Gilbert Stuart, Courtesy Bowdoin College Museum of Art, Reproduced from the *Dictionary of American
Portraits* published by Dover Publications, Inc., 1967, p. 69; Painting by Rembrandt Reale, Courtesy
Virginia Museum of Fine Arts, The Glasgow Fund, Reproduced from the *Dictionary of American Portraits*
published by Dover Publications, Inc., 1967, p. 17; Reproduced from the *Dictionary of American Portraits*
published by Dover Publications, Inc., 1967, pp. 37, 42, 48.

Cover Photos: Franz Jantzen, "Collection of the Supreme Court of the United States" (background); Corel
Corporation (inset).

Contents

1

The Journey Begins

On August 7, 1807, the steamboat *Clermont* sailed upstream from a port on the Hudson River in New York City to Albany, some 150 miles north. This was the first time a steam-powered boat had ever successfully operated. The trip to Albany took thirty-two hours. Forty passengers were on the boat. Most of them were friends and relatives of the boat's owners, Robert Fulton and Robert Livingston. Shortly after the *Clermont* returned to New York City several weeks later, Fulton wrote to one of his friends:

> The power of propelling boats by steam is now fully proved. The morning I left New York there were not perhaps thirty persons in the city who believed that the boat would ever move one mile per hour or be of the least utility. . . . I feel pleasure in reflecting on the

immense advantages that my country will draw from the invention.[1]

Fulton and Livingston could not have imagined that they were also starting a journey that would end in an important decision by the United States Supreme Court. That case would involve a special privilege, a monopoly grant, that New York lawmakers gave to Fulton and Livingston. The decision would be based on the Commerce Clause of the United States Constitution, article 1, section 8, which states: "The Congress shall have power to . . . regulate commerce with foreign nations, and among the several states, and with the Indian Tribes." The phrase that became important in the steamboat monopoly case was "among the several states."

Neither Fulton nor Livingston would be alive when the case about the steamboat monopoly, *Gibbons* v. *Ogden,* was decided by the Supreme Court in 1824. And neither Fulton nor Livingston would have any personal connection with the two people involved in the case, Thomas Gibbons and Aaron Ogden.

Nine years before the *Clermont* sailed, in 1798, New York lawmakers passed a statute (law) that granted Livingston and his business partners the right to be the only company that could operate steamboats on the lakes and rivers of that state. This exclusive privilege is called a monopoly. One condition of this particular monopoly grant was that Livingston had one year to build a boat that could actually sail. Another person had already tried to build a steam-powered boat but had failed. His name was John Fitch, and he was the actual inventor of the steamboat. He had received a similar monopoly grant the year before. When he was not able to produce a boat that worked, the lawmakers revoked his monopoly; they took it away, and they gave it to Livingston. At first, Livingston also failed to build a successful boat. However, he had many friends and family members among the lawmakers, and he persuaded

At first, Robert Livingston failed to build a successful steamboat. However, many of his friends and family members were among the lawmakers who renewed his twenty-year monopoly twice, in 1803 and again in 1807.

them to renew his twenty-year monopoly twice, first in 1803 and again in 1807, the year the *Clermont* sailed for the first time. He was finally able to produce a steam-powered boat with help from his friend and business partner, Robert Fulton.

Robert Fulton and Robert Livingston had first met each other in 1803 when they were both living in Paris, France. Fulton was artistic and interested in a variety of subjects. He had moved to Paris from New York several years before to study painting. He was a slender man who stood straight and tall. His friends said he had the eyes of a dreamer.[2] Livingston was more practical. He arrived in Paris in 1803 as a diplomatic representative of the new United States government. He and his family owned large areas of land in the state of New York. Livingston was a tall, distinguished man with a strong personality. He and Fulton soon discovered that they shared an interest in scientific experiments. They were especially interested in building boats that could be run by steam.

Fulton and Livingston soon returned to New York and established a business partnership. It was a good combination. Both men were bold and optimistic, and each had some feature the other lacked. Fulton was a skilled mechanic and a good mathematician. He was also knowledgeable about scientific theory. His partner,

Robert Fulton (shown here) was Robert Livingston's business partner. Fulton was an engineer, inventor, and pioneer in the design of steamboats.

Livingston, was very wealthy. His relatives and friends were influential in New York politics, and he knew that he could call on them if he needed a favor. And he took advantage of this situation. He asked and received favors of them several times. This was especially true when he requested extensions of his monopoly so that he and Fulton could have time to produce a steamboat that actually worked.

Both men were certain that boats powered by steam would be the most efficient way to move people and freight across long distances. The successful voyage of the *Clermont* proved that steamboats could work.

Steam is a form of water called vapor. This vapor appears in the air as a strong, misty stream. The idea of using steam as a source of power for transportation goes back to ancient Egypt. Scientists, however, were not able to actually translate the idea into reality until the late eighteenth century. On the *Clermont,* the steam originated in a huge boiler, twenty feet long. The steam then went into a large cylinder tube, where it traveled until it reached two large paddle wheels. When these paddle wheels turned, they caused the boat to move. Robert Fulton's great-granddaughter described how the machinery looked in his boat:

> [It] was an odd craft. The machinery, placed in the center, was exposed to view and creaked ominously.

Only the bow and stern were covered to form the cabins. The unprotected paddle-wheels swung ponderously at each side and splashed the water as they revolved.[3]

Everyone seemed to be enthusiastic about the possibilities of steamboat travel. The railroad had not been developed yet, so the American people could move goods or passengers long distances only by way of rivers and canals or on rough roads called turnpikes. Farmers were especially eager to find a quick, inexpensive way to transport their corn and grains to market because the teams of horses that hauled these easily spoiled crops could travel only two miles an hour.[4]

Not everyone, however, was enthusiastic about the

Livingston and Fulton were sure that steam would be the most efficient way to move people and freight across long distances. The successful voyage of the *Clermont* proved them right.

11

steamboat monopoly given to Fulton and Livingston. Many people in New York and in other states thought that the monopoly grant favored a small group of wealthy people and prevented other interested people from operating steamboats. Several nearby states, including Connecticut and New Jersey, passed laws that prohibited New York boats from traveling on their rivers. This unhappiness with the Fulton-Livingston steamboat monopoly was the start of a journey to the United States Supreme Court that would end in 1824 with the case of *Gibbons* v. *Ogden*.

2

America Becomes a Nation

When the *Clermont* first sailed in 1807, the United States was still a young nation. Many Americans could still remember the turmoil of the Revolutionary War, also known as the War for American Independence. The war was fought between the American colonists living in the thirteen original colonies and the "mother country," England. The fighting began in 1775 at the Battle of Lexington and Concord and ended in 1781 at the Battle of Yorktown.

The Revolutionary War

The American colonists fought against England and its king, George III, for many reasons. England had forced the colonies to pay taxes to finance the French and Indian War in 1763, even though the colonists were not represented in the English ruling body, Parliament, and therefore had no voice in its decisions. The colonists complained that they should have "no taxation without representation." England also tried to tell the colonists which goods they could trade and would not allow the colonists to move west. After England passed more taxes, including a tax on tea, the colonists decided to take action. They met at the first Continental Congress in Philadelphia in 1774 to protest these acts. When the Second Continental Congress met, in May 1775, the fighting had already begun. The Americans appointed General George Washington to lead their troops. Later, he would be elected America's first president. In July 1776, delegates to the Second Continental Congress wrote the Declaration of Independence. The Americans declared their freedom from England. The war was not officially over, however, until 1783, when the new United States of America and England signed the Treaty of Paris.

Those Americans who had lived through the war believed that the younger generation would soon forget how hard the colonists had fought for independence from England. The Revolutionary War generation was especially worried that the younger generation would be careless about protecting their new freedoms.

The War of 1812

In 1812 another war with England broke out. The War of 1812 has also been called the second American war for independence. The main cause of this war was the fact that the British were violating American shipping rights. The British were forcing American sailors to serve on British ships. During the war the British burned the White House and several other buildings in Washington, D.C. It was also during this war that the national anthem of the United States, "The Star-Spangled Banner," was written by Francis Scott Key. He composed it after he saw the American flag still flying over Fort McHenry in Maryland after an attack by British troops.

When the war ended in 1815, with an American victory, a huge growth spurt occurred in the country. New states were added to the Union, the economy expanded, and people moved westward. One historian has said that "Americans basked in a sense of victory. . . . A spirit of energy invigorated the nation, and there could be no doubt that a nation now existed."[1]

Many people, however, were frightened that America was becoming too much of a single nation and that the individual states were losing their identity. These people were known as states' rights supporters. One target of their distrust was the United States Supreme Court, especially its fourth Chief Justice, John Marshall. Chief Justice Marshall was in favor of a strong central government. Supporters of a strong central government were called nationalists.

John Marshall

Chief Justice John Marshall was appointed to the Supreme Court by President John Adams in 1801. Marshall was born in Fauquier County, Virginia, in 1755, the oldest of fifteen children. Virginia was one of the original thirteen colonies. At the time of Marshall's birth, Virginia was "a thinly settled, stable but expansive agricultural society with well-defined classes and a firm attachment to government by the rich, the well-born, and the able. . . . [L]and was the springboard to political influence."[2] A man could not vote or hold political office in Virginia unless he owned land. (No women were allowed to vote or hold political office.)

John Marshall's father was a lawyer, and he taught his son the law. Most lawyers during that time did not have formal law school training, but rather "read" law; they studied with an experienced lawyer. As a young man, Marshall frequently accompanied his father to

Chief Justice John Marshall was a nationalist—someone in favor of a strong central government.

court and also joined him at political meetings in Fauquier County. One of Marshall's biographers has written that through these activities "he acquired the manners and habits of a Virginia gentleman—a sense of duty, a fondness for games and athletic contests, a gracious hospitality, and a disarming, engaging personality."[3]

When the Revolutionary War broke out, John Marshall and his father were among the first men in Virginia to join as soldiers.[4] Marshall fought in several important battles in Virginia and the surrounding area. During the winter of 1777–1778 he was stationed at Valley Forge, Pennsylvania. The weather was especially cold, and the troops had hardly any food, clothing, shoes, or supplies. Several years after the war, Marshall described the terrible conditions:

> At no period of the war had the situation of the American army been more perilous than at Valley Forge. Even when the troops were not entirely destitute of food, their stock of provisions was so scanty that a quantity sufficient for one week was scarcely in store. . . . Scarcely one man . . . had a pair of shoes.[5]

Many of the soldiers blamed these bad conditions on the Second Continental Congress, which was the central government in charge of the war. Most historians believe that it was during this long, cold winter at

Valley Forge that John Marshall decided that a strong, powerful national government was necessary for the United States.[6] Later, during the war, Marshall served as a deputy judge advocate, or legal adviser to one of the army commanders.

After the war, John Marshall returned to Virginia. He attended law lectures at the College of William and Mary for three months. Then, he set up a law practice in Richmond, where he moved with his wife and family. He soon developed a reputation as an outstanding lawyer, and he still found time to be active in political activities. In 1788 a convention was held in each state to ratify (approve) the Constitution of the United States. Marshall was a delegate to the Virginia convention. He made many speeches on the convention floor, asking the delegates to support the proposed Constitution. Supporters of the Constitution were called Federalists. Many delegates were opposed to the document because they were afraid that it gave too much power to the national government. When the vote was taken, the Federalists won by a narrow margin. Marshall's home was within walking distance of the convention hall, and he often provided food and wine for the delegates. His wife, Polly, was frequently ill, so Marshall took care of the arrangements himself.[7]

Soon Marshall became known outside Virginia. In

1797 President John Adams appointed him as one of three negotiators to France. They were supposed to settle a scandal, but they were unsuccessful. The scandal involved three French agents who tried to bribe some American representatives who were attempting to negotiate a treaty with France. Marshall was also elected as a representative to Congress from Virginia. He served from 1799 to 1800. At the time of his appointment to the Supreme Court, he was secretary of state in President Adams's administration.

A few years after his appointment, one of his colleagues, Justice Joseph Story, described him in a letter to a friend:

> Marshall is of a tall, slender figure, not graceful, nor imposing. His eyes small and twinkling, his forehead rather low, but his features are in general harmonious. His manners are plain, yet dignified; and an unaffected modesty diffuses itself through all his actions. His dress is very simple, yet neat. . . . His genius is, in my opinion, vigorous and powerful. . . . He examines the intricacies of a subject with calm and perserving acuteness. . . .[8]

Historians believe that Marshall was one of the most influential Chief Justices who ever sat on the Court.[9] His interpretations of the Constitution strengthened the roles of the Supreme Court and the federal government.

Branches of Government

The federal government consists of three branches: the executive, the legislative, and the judicial. These branches were established in the Constitution, the fundamental law of the United States, which went into effect in 1789. The executive branch includes the president, the vice-president, and the Cabinet. The president and vice-president are elected by the voters of the United States, and the Cabinet is appointed by the president. This branch is responsible for seeing that the work of the other two branches is carried out. The executive branch also suggests legislation to Congress and appoints members of the Supreme Court and the lower federal courts. The legislative branch is made up of the two houses of Congress, the Senate, and the House of Representatives. This branch is elected by the voters. Its main job is to pass laws. It also confirms the president's appointments of judges to the federal courts, including the Supreme Court. The judicial branch is made up of the Supreme Court and the lower federal courts. Its main duty is to interpret laws passed by the legislative branch, to make sure that they conform to the Constitution.

The Constitution also established a system of government in which power is divided between a national or federal government and the states. This system is called federalism. Each state also has three branches of government: the executive, the legislative, and the judicial. The state executive is the governor, who is elected by the voters of each state, and his or her Cabinet. The legislative branch is called the legislature or, in some states, the assembly. These lawmakers' main job is to pass laws for that particular state. The judicial branch is made up of state judges, including a state Supreme Court. Its job is to interpret acts of the lawmakers. The states can pass, enforce, and interpret their own laws so long as they do not violate the United States Constitution. The states' power to pass certain laws would be an important issue in the steamboat monopoly case, *Gibbons* v. *Ogden.*

John Marshall believed that a strong national government was necessary to prevent the new nation from breaking up into factions, also called special interest groups. He also believed that the Supreme Court was the branch of government that could make sure this did not happen.

Before John Marshall became Chief Justice, the Supreme Court was the least important of the three branches of government. Some of Marshall's predecessors seemed not to take their job very seriously. The first Chief Justice, John Jay, resigned to become governor of New York; he even campaigned for that office while he was still a member of the Court. When he was Chief Justice, he also found enough time to serve as America's ambassador to England. The Chief Justice who served immediately before Marshall, Oliver Ellsworth, resigned after only four years. He did not think that the job was interesting or important enough. Frequently, the six Justices (there were seven after 1807; today there are nine) each wrote separate opinions on the cases they heard. And in some years the Court did not hear any cases at all.

John Marshall changed the work of the Court. Under his leadership, the Court spoke as a unified body, even though some of the other Justices occasionally presented dissenting (opposing) opinions. Although the other Justices frequently wrote the opinions issued by the Court, Marshall wrote the majority of them during the years when he served as Chief Justice.

One of Marshall's most important achievements was the fact that he established the principle of judicial review. This principle says that the courts can declare acts of the executive or legislative branches unconstitutional. This idea came about in the Court's ruling in a case called *Marbury* v. *Madison* in 1803.[10] Another of Marshall's important achievements was his ruling that the Supreme Court can declare acts of state lawmakers to be unconstitutional. This would be an important issue in *Gibbons* v. *Ogden*. The Marshall Court decided several cases that announced these principles in the years before it heard *Gibbons*. These decisions angered states' rights supporters, who believed that the Court would cause the states to become insignificant.

Fletcher v. *Peck*

Fletcher v. *Peck*, one such case, was decided in 1810.[11] This was the first time that the Supreme Court declared a state law unconstitutional. The law in question had been passed by the Georgia state lawmakers. The lawmakers had repealed (withdrawn) a law passed by the previous lawmakers. Under the original law, Georgia had sold several million acres of land at a low price to four land speculator companies. Land speculators bought land and hoped to sell it at a higher price when the value of the land rose. The speculators had promised some lawmakers that they would make money from these lands. The next elected group of lawmakers correctly believed that this was bribery. They voted to overturn the original law. However, many of the people who had purchased the land after the law was repealed realized that they might now own the land illegally. Robert Fletcher was one of these people. He sued John Peck, the man who sold him the land. The case was brought to the United States Supreme Court on the grounds that Georgia lawmakers had broken a contract when they repealed the original law.

The Court, in an opinion written by John Marshall, ruled that the Georgia lawmakers had violated the Contract Clause of the Constitution when they over-turned the original land grant law. The Contract Clause (Article I, section 10) provides that "No state shall . . . pass any law impairing the obligation of contracts." Marshall said that a land grant was a contract, and the lawmakers had broken that contract. The fact that the land buyers and the lawmakers were involved in cor-ruption and bribery did not matter. An act passed by state lawmakers would also be an issue in *Gibbons* v. *Ogden* fourteen years later.

Martin v. Hunter's Lessee

Meanwhile, the Supreme Court heard another case involving land claims. This case came from Virginia, John Marshall's home state. The issue was whether a foreign-born man could inherit land in the state in which he lived. (Women could not inherit land.) The Virginia state court said no, but in 1813 the Supreme Court disagreed and overturned the state court's decision.[12] Virginians felt that the Supreme Court had interfered in their state business.

25

In 1816 in another case about disputed lands, the state of Virginia challenged a section of the Judiciary Act of 1789. This act of Congress had established the structure and duties of the federal courts. In this case, *Martin v. Hunter's Lessee,* the state of Virginia argued that a section of the Judiciary Act was unconstitutional.[13] The section in question gave the Supreme Court the authority to rule on decisions of a state's highest court when federal laws or treaties were involved. Virginians believed that this provision gave the Court too much power over the states. John Marshall abstained from (did not participate in) the decision. He felt he had a conflict of interest because some of the disputed lands had been bought by his brother.

The Court's opinion was written by Justice Joseph Story. Historians consider him to be almost as important a Justice as Marshall. He was one of the most articulate members of the Court at that time.[14] The Court ruled that the Judiciary Act of 1789 was constitutional. The decision stated that when the American people adopted the Constitution, they created a single nation and gave the federal courts exclusive power over national judicial issues. Story's opinion has been called "a landmark in the history of federal judicial supremacy."[15] Several years later, in *Gibbons,* state court decisions would also be important.

Two more cases that came before *Gibbons* convinced some people that states' rights were being completely eliminated.

Dartmouth College v. Woodward

One case in 1819 was again based on the Contract Clause of the Constitution. This time, the contract was between a state and a state college that had been chartered (established) as a corporation. New Hampshire lawmakers had tried to change the charter they had given to Dartmouth College many years before. In *Dartmouth College* v. *Woodward*, Marshall wrote that, once again, a state had broken a contract, even though the Constitution stated that it had no right to do so.[16] The state had no right to change anything in the charter it had given to Dartmouth College unless the college also agreed to the change.

McCulloch v. Maryland

Another important case, *McCulloch* v. *Maryland*, was decided that same year.[17] The Court ruled that the state of Maryland did not have the right to tax the Second Bank of the United States. The Second Bank was a national bank that Congress had established three years earlier. Many Americans disliked the bank, and several states attempted to prevent it from opening branches.

When that strategy failed, some states tried to place such a high tax on the branches that they could not afford to stay open. That is what Maryland had done. James McCulloch, a bank cashier in Baltimore, refused to pay the tax. He said it was unconstitutional for the state to tax a national bank. On the other side, lawyers for Maryland claimed that Congress had overstepped its powers when it established the bank. They said that a state could tax any bank located within its borders.

When the case reached the Supreme Court, Daniel Webster argued on the side of the bank. (A few years later he would be one of the lawyers involved in *Gibbons* v. *Ogden.*) Webster argued the power to tax can be "a power to destroy." Since the bank was an agency of the United States government, a state that tried to put the bank out of business by taxing it was, in effect, trying to destroy the federal government.

John Marshall and the Supreme Court ruled that Congress had the authority to charter a bank, even though the Constitution said nothing about it. Marshall based his decision on the implied powers doctrine. This doctrine arose out of Article I, section 8 of the Constitution, which enumerates (lists) specific powers of Congress. The doctrine of implied powers allows Congress to exercise authority that is *implied,* or suggested, by these specific grants of powers. Marshall wrote that Congress did not have specific power under the Constitution to establish a national bank. It did, however, have the power to tax and to regulate commerce. Therefore, he said, "a government entrusted with such ample powers, on the due execution of which the happiness and prosperity of the nation so vitally depends, must also be entrusted with ample means for their execution."[18] The power to regulate commerce would be a very important issue in *Gibbons.*

The *McCulloch* decision drew national attention. Newspapers all over the country published the text of the entire opinion. The decision was popular in the northern states, but very unpopular in the South, especially in Virginia and Maryland.

In just a few short years, the steamboat monopoly case would also draw national attention. Two of these same issues would be argued again in *Gibbons* v. *Ogden:* whether the Supreme Court had the power to declare state laws unconstitutional, and how far the Court could go in interpreting the Constitution, especially the Commerce Clause.

3

The Road to the Supreme Court

Aaron Ogden, a resident of New Jersey, wanted to be in the steamboat business. In 1813, when he was fifty-seven years old, he had already lived an active life. He had been a soldier in the Revolutionary War, a successful lawyer, a United States senator from New Jersey, and then governor of that state. Ogden built a steamboat called the *Sea Horse* and began ferrying passengers between New Jersey and New York. This business was illegal because he was in competition with the Fulton-Livingston monopoly. A New York court had just decided a case that upheld the monopoly.[1] Ogden, however, saw no reason that the state of New York should tell him what to do.

The terms of the Fulton-Livingston monopoly prevented ships from Ogden's home state of New Jersey from entering New York ports. In 1811 New Jersey lawmakers had passed a law that gave the citizens of that state the right to own and operate steamboats on all the waters between New Jersey and New York, despite what the New York monopoly law said. Then, in 1813, New Jersey lawmakers passed their own monopoly law. Ogden had many friends who were lawmakers, and they worked on his behalf to pass a law that gave him the exclusive right to operate steamboats from most ports in New Jersey to New York City. The law would be in effect for two years or until New York repealed its law. This law also gave the state of New Jersey the authority to capture any steamboats from New York that were sailing on rivers or lakes in New Jersey.

Two years later, however, the New Jersey lawmakers, after a long and heated debate, voted by a one-vote margin to end Ogden's monopoly. He lost because the lawmakers who were his friends were no longer in the majority party. Ogden had lost his chance to defy the New York monopoly.

Ogden then went to New York and spoke to a committee of lawmakers. He urged the lawmakers to repeal the Fulton-Livingston monopoly grant. Ogden emphasized what he thought was one of the most unfair provisions of the grant: Although New York authorities had the power to seize illegal boats, they were not required to pay any money to the boats' owners.

Ogden's request to repeal the monopoly was referred to a New York state senate committee. The committee's chairman had once been a business partner of Robert Livingston. The two men had had a disagreement, however, and the chairman was now opposed to the monopoly. The committee recommended to all the lawmakers that the law be changed. The committee's final report mentioned that the power over interstate commerce, that is, business between states, belonged to the national government rather than to the states. Ten years later, Chief Justice John Marshall based his opinion on the same point when the Supreme Court heard the steamboat monopoly case. New York lawmakers, however, ignored the committee's advice and allowed the monopoly to remain in effect.

Ogden did not give up. He still wanted to be in the steamboat business, so he bought a license to operate boats from the owners of the Fulton-Livingston monopoly. Robert Livingston had recently died, and Robert Fulton would die a few years later, but the New York law was written so that their heirs would continue to hold the monopoly. Other people could operate steamboats by paying a fee to the monopoly owners.

Aaron Ogden was a resident of New Jersey who wanted to be in the steamboat business. He bought a license to operate steamboats from the owners of the Fulton-Livingston monopoly.

This is similar to someone today buying a franchise from a company to operate a store or fast-food restaurant. By paying five hundred dollars a year to Fulton's and Livingston's heirs, Aaron Ogden was allowed to operate his steamboats between Elizabethtown (now Elizabeth), New Jersey, and the ports of New York.

There had been a great deal of opposition to the Fulton-Livingston monopoly in New York even before Aaron Ogden came along. After the successful launch of the *Clermont* in 1807 showed that steamboats could be an efficient form of transportation, many people wanted to get into the steamboat business. The only way they could do so, however, was to purchase a license from the Fulton-Livingston monopoly. Fulton and Livingston were apparently surprised at the negative reaction to their monopoly grant.

> Although they had shown true vision in their estimate of the steamboat's future, Livingston and Fulton had been somewhat less perceptive in gauging the reaction of their countrymen. They had not supposed that their monopoly would be unpopular. . . .[2]

Challenging the Monopoly

One of the challengers was James Van Ingen. A few years before Aaron Ogden came on the scene, Van Ingen started running competing steamboats on the Hudson River. Fulton and Livingston took action immediately. They asked a New York court for an injunction against Van Ingen. An injunction is an order from a court to prohibit a person from performing a specific act. Van Ingen's attorney objected to the injunction. He claimed that his client had as much right as Fulton, Livingston, or anyone else to operate steamboats. He argued that the monopoly statute was unconstitutional. On the other side, Fulton and Livingston's attorneys argued that the lawmakers had the authority to grant a monopoly. The court denied the injunction, relying on an ancient English law that said the public had a common right to the air and, most important in this situation, the sea. Fulton and Livingston had lost this round.

Fulton and Livingston appealed the decision against them to the highest New York court of appeals, then called the New York Court of Errors. This court was unusual. Even though New York had modeled its government on the federal division of three branches—the legislative, the executive, and the judicial—this court was made up of the five judges of the state Supreme Court and the state senators. The Court of Errors reversed the lower court. It upheld the injunction against Van Ingen. This decision was not surprising, because many of the senators on the court had, in their capacity as lawmakers, also voted to pass the monopoly statute.

The judge based his decision on the concurrent powers argument. This principle states that although Congress and the states each had exclusive authority to make laws in some areas, they also had authority to make the same laws in other areas. This argument would surface again when the Supreme Court heard *Gibbons* v. *Ogden.*

Once again a court had decided that the steamboat monopoly was legal. Meanwhile, Aaron Ogden had acquired a business partner, Thomas Gibbons. Gibbons and Ogden had similar backgrounds. Gibbons had also been a soldier in the Revolutionary War but on the Loyalist (British) side. He had also held political office; he was mayor of Savannah, Georgia, in the 1790s

Thomas Gibbons (shown here) eventually became Aaron Ogden's business partner.

before he moved to New Jersey. It is unclear how he and Ogden met, but the two men shared an interest in owning and operating steamboats.

The Partners Separate

The partnership soon broke up, however. Part of the reason may have been the men's personalities. Gibbons has been described as "self-centered, hot-headed, and rather slippery."[3]

Ogden, too, often acted impulsively. Near the end of their partnership, Ogden had Gibbons arrested, without warning, because Gibbons had failed to pay back an overdue loan. The final blow for the partnership had nothing to do with the steamboat business, however. The break occurred when Ogden became involved in an argument between Gibbons and Gibbons's wife. The quarrel involved the reputation of Gibbons's daughter. Ogden sided with the mother and daughter against Gibbons. One day, while the dispute was going on, Gibbons picked up a horsewhip, went to Ogden's home, and threatened to beat him. Ogden ran out his back door and escaped over a fence. When he returned home, he discovered that Gibbons had posted a notice on Ogden's gate describing what a terrible person Ogden was. Ogden then sued Gibbons for trespass (being on his property illegally).

He was awarded twenty-five hundred dollars by a judge.

Gibbons Competes With Ogden

Shortly after this incident, in 1817, Thomas Gibbons started a competing steamboat business close to Ogden's base of operations. Gibbons bought a small steamboat and then a larger one. He also found a new business partner, Cornelius Vanderbilt. Vanderbilt came from a wealthy, prominent New York family and many years later would become the force behind America's railroad empire. Vanderbilt had the energy and financial know-how necessary to make Gibbons's steamboat business profitable in a very short time. He convinced Gibbons to provide lower rates and better service than his competitors could provide. Vanderbilt was also ruthless and had no qualms about defying the hated New York monopoly. Soon this competing business began cutting into Ogden's profits.

Aaron Ogden was angry, so he went to court to try to stop Gibbons's competing business. In October 1818, he asked for an injunction against Gibbons. The New York Court of Chancery issued a preliminary, or temporary, injunction against Gibbons. Courts of chancery were common in the nineteenth century. These courts administered justice according to rules of

Gibbons and Ogden eventually ended their business partnership, and Cornelius Vanderbilt (shown here) became Gibbons's new business partner.

equity or fairness rather than following the strict rules of the law. Meanwhile, the court's chancellor, its chief judge, James Kent, studied the matter, and Gibbons and Ogden prepared their cases.

Gibbons and his attorneys argued against the preliminary injunction. They brought up an interesting point that would later be important when the Supreme Court heard the case: Gibbons had a license to run his steamboats that was issued under the United States Coasting Act of 1783. That license, because it was issued by the federal government, proved that Congress, rather than an individual state, had the authority to regulate steamboat travel on interstate waterways. Chancellor Kent, however, said that the only purpose of this license was to provide money and to designate ships as American. He ruled that New York had the authority to grant monopolies and that, therefore, Gibbons was operating his business illegally.

Kent then issued a permanent injunction against Thomas Gibbons. He ruled that Gibbons could not legally operate his boats anywhere in New York. Only people operating under the Fulton-Livingston monopoly had a right to do so. This was not the first time Kent had ruled on a suit over the monopoly. Six years before, in 1812, he had decided another case in favor of that monopoly.[4]

Despite the injunction, Gibbons's business partner, Cornelius Vanderbilt, continued to sail one of his boats, the *Bellona*, around New York whenever he pleased. In 1817 the vice-president of the United States, Daniel Tompkins, also became involved. Tompkins was a former governor of New York. He evidently used his New York political connections and his friendship with Vanderbilt to make it possible for Gibbons's boats to land at Staten Island in New York City, where the passengers could transfer to other boats and continue their trips to various New York ports.

So Ogden went back to court to stop Gibbons from operating his boats in New York waters. Chancellor

Daniel Tompkins (shown here), a former governor of New York and former vice-president of the United States, used his New York political connections to allow Gibbons's boats to land in Staten Island, New York. Passengers could then transfer to other boats and continue their trips to other New York ports.

Kent issued another injunction against Gibbons. This injunction also ordered Gibbons to break off his arrangement with Daniel Tompkins.

Gibbons appealed his injunction to the New York Court of Errors. (New York had several layers of courts.) In 1820 this court ruled that the state of New York had the right to grant a steamboat monopoly.[5] Gibbons had lost again.

He had one last chance to stop the Fulton-Livingston monopoly. He and his lawyers appealed his case to the United States Supreme Court. This means that they asked the highest court in the nation to hear his case.

The Supreme Court's job is to review decisions from state and lower federal courts. In *Gibbons* v. *Ogden*, the Justices reviewed a case from a New York state court. When they review a decision, the Justices look at the lower court's decisions to determine whether they agree with the Constitution and the laws of the United States. When Thomas Gibbons's attorneys appealed his case to the Supreme Court, they had no guarantee that the Court would hear the case. So many cases are appealed each year that the Justices have to determine which of them are important enough to review. The number of cases that the Court has to consider has grown each year. During its first decade, 1791–1800, the Court had little business; it heard only about one hundred cases during the entire decade. The number grew in the nineteenth and twentieth centuries. Today, some four to five thousand cases are appealed to the Supreme Court each term, but the Justices usually agree to hear fewer than two hundred.[6]

Thomas Gibbons was lucky. The Supreme Court decided to hear his appeal.

4

The Case for Thomas Gibbons

Attorneys Daniel Webster and William Wirt arrived in Washington, D.C., on February 4, 1824, to argue Thomas Gibbons's case before the United States Supreme Court. They found a very different city from the one we know today. Our nation's capital was then a little more than thirty years old, and it still looked unfinished. The streets were unpaved, and after a hard rain, they resembled a muddy swamp. Members of Congress and the Supreme Court Justices lived in temporary quarters in boardinghouses near the Capitol. As soon as Congress or the Court finished a term, the members immediately returned to their home states.

The Supreme Court also was a very different

institution from the Court we know today. Now, the Court meets and has its offices in an impressive marble building. The nine Justices hear cases and announce their decisions in an elegant courtroom. They have ample space for their chambers—private offices—and facilities for their law clerks and other staff, as well as a large library. In the 1820s, however, the Supreme Court occupied one room in the basement of the yet unfinished Capitol, under the Senate chamber. The seven Justices did not have private offices or a staff. They usually discussed cases and other Court business while they ate their meals together in the boardinghouses where they lived. A New York newspaper reporter described the facilities on the opening day of the *Gibbons* hearing:

> The [courtroom] is not in a style which comports with the dignity of that body, or which wears a comparison with the other Halls of the Capitol. In the first place, it is like going down cellar [in the basement] to reach it. The room is on the basement story in an obscure part of the north wing. . . . A stranger might traverse the dark avenues of the Capitol for a week without finding the remote room in which Justice is administered to the American Republic.[1]

Today, the Supreme Court meets from the first Monday in October through June. In the 1820s, the Court met for only a few months, sometimes for only six weeks in a whole year. The sessions were usually in the winter. *Gibbons* was argued on the first day of the 1824 term, February 4.

The case came before the Court earlier in the 1824 term than any of the parties had anticipated. It was initially case number 29 on the Court docket (the list of cases to be heard) when the Court convened for that term. It was called up much earlier, however, because the attorneys for the other cases on the list were not prepared to present their arguments. Thomas Gibbons's attorneys were prepared to present their case, but they, too, had to scramble at the last minute. One of the attorneys, William Wirt, admitted at the time that "I have . . . yet to study the case; but I know the facts, and have only to weave the argument."[2]

Neither of Gibbons's attorneys were strangers to Washington, D.C., or to the legal system. Daniel Webster was a member of Congress from the state of Massachusetts. William Wirt was the attorney general (the chief law officer) of the United States. Unlike today, government officials in the 1820s could represent their clients at the Supreme Court. Today, this would be considered a conflict of interest.

Almost any other man would have been physically exhausted had he followed forty-two-year-old Daniel Webster's schedule the night before he made his opening argument to the Court. Webster had stayed up

The Fulton-Livingston steamboat monopoly marked the beginning of a journey that ended with the United States Supreme Court's 1824 decision in *Gibbons* v. *Ogden*.

the whole night preparing his brief (oral argument). He worked eleven hours on it. Then he went to his barber for a shave—a common practice in those days—and ate a light breakfast of tea and crackers. This all-night session evidently did not bother Webster. Years later he told one of his biographers that he thought he "never on any occasion had so completely the free use of his faculties."[3]

Daniel Webster's Arguments

Webster was a big man with a booming voice. He loved to talk and had a reputation as a great public speaker. Appearing before the Supreme Court gave him an opportunity to show off his skills. He spent two and a half hours arguing his case before the Justices. Today attorneys who appear before the Supreme Court are required to limit their arguments to thirty minutes, but in the 1820s there was no time limit. (Aaron Ogden's attorneys took even longer to present their arguments.)

Webster emphatically told the Court that the New York steamboat monopoly was unconstitutional because it regulated interstate commerce. He insisted that only Congress had the authority to do that. Article I, section 8 of the United States Constitution supported his argument. This clause gives Congress the power to "regulate Commerce with foreign Nations, and among the several States, and with the Indian Tribes."

Webster began his argument by pointing out that New York lawmakers had indeed enacted a monopoly grant for the past twenty-five years. When the law was challenged, it was upheld in New York courts.[4] A less confident attorney would not have even mentioned this, but Webster had a deliberate reason for doing so: He wanted to lecture the Court about its proper role. He reminded the Justices that the Constitution gave them the power to look at what the state lawmakers and state courts had decided and to reverse those decisions if they believed them to be unconstitutional. This power was exactly what states' rights supporters disliked so much. Webster was a true nationalist, a staunch supporter of federal control over certain areas of state and federal law.

Now Webster came to the heart of his argument: that the steamboat monopoly law passed by New York lawmakers was unconstitutional. It was a definite regulation of interstate commerce. This was something that only Congress had the power to do. He insisted that the New York courts had acted incorrectly when they upheld the monopoly law.

Webster then gave the Court a brief history lesson. He talked about how the use of steamboats had grown over the years, traveling along rivers that formed boundaries between states. He emphasized that if several states all passed monopoly statutes, there would soon be a confusing jumble of laws and regulations. Inevitably, one state's regulations would be hostile to another's. He asked: If any one of these laws were valid, would any "point out where the state right stopped?"[5] This is why, Webster told the Court, the Constitution gave the national government authority to act alone in certain areas. Any other interpretation would result in confusion: The power of Congress to regulate commerce was complete and entire, and, to a certain extent,

Daniel Webster, one of Gibbons's attorneys, was a member of Congress from the state of Massachusetts. He had a reputation as an excellent public speaker.

necessary and exclusive; and the acts in question were regulations of commerce.[6]

Next, he pointed out that Congress and the states had two kinds of powers: exclusive power, which meant that each had specific unique powers in certain areas, and concurrent power, which meant that each had authority to make laws on the same subject in certain areas. He argued that the Constitution definitely did not establish concurrent powers relating to interstate commerce. Once again, he gave the Court a brief history lesson. He pointed out that when the Constitution was adopted, the framers especially wanted to eliminate a possibility for each state to act as if it were an independent country:

> We do not find in the history of the formation and adoption of the Constitution, that any man speaks of a general *concurrent* power, in the regulation of foreign and domestic trade, as still residing in the States. The very object intended, more than any other, was to take away such power. If it had not been so provided, the Constitution would not have ben worth accepting.[7]

Webster next attacked an interpretation of the Federal Coasting Act of 1793 that Chancellor James Kent had made when he ruled to uphold the New York monopoly. Kent had said that Thomas Gibbons's license to operate steamboats, which he held under the United States Coasting Act of 1793, was just a measure to provide money for the government. Instead, Webster said, this license gave Gibbons the right to "navigate freely the waters of the United States."[8] The monopoly grant that New York had given to Aaron Ogden, however, prevented his client, Thomas Gibbons, from doing so.

Webster had called forth all his speaking skills. The audience who came to watch him praised him highly. A reporter covering the case for a Washington newspaper called his argument "one of the most powerful arguments we ever have heard."[9]

In contrast to Daniel Webster's dramatic performance, William Wirt's presentation was more low-key. Although a brilliant and well-respected attorney, Wirt lacked Webster's public-speaking flair.

In his presentation, Wirt argued that Congress had exclusive power over interstate commerce and that any challenge to that supremacy was unconstitutional. His one moment of drama came in his closing statement: He pleaded for an end to the hostility between the states caused by the monopoly laws before a civil war started.

5

The Case for Aaron Ogden

Aaron Ogden's two attorneys were well known and well respected. Thomas Oakley spoke first. He had been the attorney general for the state of New York. He was not, however, Ogden's first choice to be his lawyer. William Pinkney, a brilliant attorney, had represented Ogden in the cases leading to the Supreme Court. He had, however, died two years earlier. Oakley was considered to be an outstanding attorney. However, he has been described as "a cold, clear reasoner, and carefully trained lawyer, but lacking imagination, warmth, or breadth of vision."[1] He was not an adequate substitute for the masterful and glowing Pinkney.[2] Evidently, he based his case to a great extent on briefs (written arguments) that Pinkney had prepared for the lower court cases.[3]

Thomas Oakley's Arguments

Oakley had a reputation for talking for as long as people would let him. Oakley took full advantage of the fact that there was no time limit imposed on his arguments. His oral argument lasted a day and a half. The written text filled eighty pages of the official court reporter, where briefs and decisions were printed.

Oakley was not intimidated by the brilliance and reputation of the attorneys for the other side, Daniel Webster and William Wirt. Nor was he intimidated by Chief Justice John Marshall or the other six Justices who sat on the bench and listened. Rather, according to a newspaper reporter, Oakley immediately "set about attacking the ramparts of the law which had just been erected with his usual coolness and deliberation."[4]

He tried to prove that it was constitutional for states to grant monopolies such as the one under which Ogden operated. Congress and the states had both exclusive and concurrent powers. Daniel Webster had also mentioned concurrent powers, but Oakley took a different point of view than that of Webster's. In contrast to Webster's, Oakley argued that both Congress and the states had concurrent power over interstate commerce.

Thomas Oakley, one of the attorneys for Aaron Ogden, tried to prove to the members of the Supreme Court that it was constitutional for states to grant monopolies such as the one under which Aaron Ogden operated. This is what the Court building looks like today.

He backed up this argument by pointing out that when the colonies declared their independence from England, they had established independent states with the authority to carry out many functions. One of these functions was regulation of commerce. Because New York was an independent state, Oakley insisted: "There are no restrictions on the power which in any manner relate to the present controversy."[5] This point was the exact opposite of what Daniel Webster had argued.

57

Oakley then pointed out that New York lawmakers were well within their authority to grant steamboat monopolies to whomever they pleased. Such a law was nothing more than a state's regulating commerce within its borders. He said that this monopoly grant:

> applies only to the waters with the State. It does not deny the right to any vessel navigated by steam; it only forbids such vessels from within its waters . . . to be moved by steam; but that vessel may still navigate by all other means. . . . It is, therefore, strictly a regulation of internal trade and navigation . . . which belongs to the State.[6]

The second attorney for Aaron Ogden was Thomas Emmet. He was unhappy that the case was being heard much earlier than it had been scheduled. He wanted the case delayed until the Court's newest Justice, Smith Thompson, had taken his seat on the bench.[7] He asked Justice Joseph Story to get the case postponed, but Story refused to help him.

Thomas Emmet's Arguments

The main point of Emmet's presentation was an extension of Oakley's argument: that a state has the power to regulate commerce within its borders. He spent several hours discussing the intricacies of the Commerce Clause of the Constitution and the way it related to state activity. His conclusion was that New

Attorneys for Aaron Ogden asked Justice Joseph Story (shown here) to have the case postponed until the Court's newest Justice, Smith Thompson, had taken his seat on the bench, but Story refused.

York lawmakers had the authority to grant a steamboat monopoly if they chose to do so.

He also pointed out, as Webster had done, that New York lawmakers had repeatedly passed the monopoly law each time they gave Fulton and Livingston an extension. The New York state courts had repeatedly upheld the law. Webster had used this point to remind the Justices that they had a duty to overrule state laws if they believed they were unconstitutional. Emmet, however, used this point to show that the Court should assume the law was constitutional because the lawmakers and the courts acted the way they did.

Emmet, like Oakley, emphasized that the states and Congress had concurrent power. In this particular situation, therefore, both Congress and the state of New York could pass laws dealing with steamboat traffic. He argued that it was unimportant whether the power to regulate commerce was exclusive or concurrent. The New York monopoly grant, he argued, did not interfere with any congressional regulation of commerce: The state was only managing its own internal affairs. He further argued that giving the federal government the exclusive power to regulate commerce would "wreck" the states. This emotional argument was the same one that states' rights supporters had always used.

Emmet spoke emotionally during his final argument.

He passionately described the many social and economic benefits that Fulton's steamboat invention had given New York. He pleaded with the Court not to destroy the lives of widows, orphans, and hardworking heads of families who depended on the success of an efficient steamboat company. He finished by saying:

> The state of New York by a patient and forbearing patronage of ten years to Livingston and Fulton . . . has called into existence the noblest and most useful improvement of the present day . . . New York may raise her head . . . and case her eyes over the whole civilization of the world.[8]

The attorneys for Aaron Ogden insisted that the state of New York had the right to grant him a steamboat monopoly. They argued that either a state or Congress could regulate interstate commerce. The attorneys for Thomas Gibbons insisted that only Congress had that power. They argued that, therefore, the monopoly was unconstitutional. Now it was up to the Supreme Court to decide.

6

The Decision

The chamber of the United States Supreme Court was crowded on March 2, 1824. Spectators moved around in excited anticipation. This was the day the Justices would announce their decision in *Gibbons* v. *Ogden.*[1] The spectators seemed to be aware of the importance of the decision. This would be the first time that the Court had a case based on the Commerce Clause of the Constitution. Attorneys for both sides had presented two main questions for the Court to answer:

1. Did Congress have power under the Commerce Clause of the Constitution to regulate navigation?

2. If Congress had that power under the Commerce Clause, was that power supreme, or did the states also have power in that area?

When Chief Justice John Marshall entered the courtroom, he was not his usual robust, energetic self. Two weeks before, on February 19, he had fallen on the ice, coming home from eating dinner at the White House. He had injured his head and dislocated his shoulder. He had actually been unconscious for several minutes after he fell. Now the sixty-nine-year-old Justice still had his arm in a sling, and he looked frail. This was his first public appearance since the accident. Several days after he fell he had written to his wife, Polly:

> Old men do not get over sprains and hurts as quickly as young ones. Although I feel no pain when perfectly still, yet I cannot get up and move about without difficulty, and cannot put on my coat. Of course I cannot go to Court.[2]

The announcement of the decision had been delayed for almost two weeks. Today, several months go by between the day the attorneys present their oral arguments and the day the Court announces its decision. That length of time was quite a bit shorter in the 1820s.

The Justices' Opinions

Marshall walked slowly and painfully to his chair behind the rail that separated the Justices from the audience. The Justices sat behind individual mahogany desks, rather than on a row of chairs behind a long table (called the bench) as they do today. Five other Justices soon joined Marshall. The newest Justice, Smith Thompson, was absent. As a newly appointed Justice who took his seat on the bench on February 10, 1824, he did not participate in the *Gibbons* case, which was argued prior to that date. He was a brother-in-law of the late Robert Livingston and had recently been appointed. His daughter had died shortly after he was sworn in, however, and he had not yet taken his seat on the Court. In fact, his absence was one reason Thomas Emmet, one of Aaron Ogden's attorneys, had tried to get the case postponed to a later date.

The other Justices were William Johnson, Joseph Story, Bushrod Washington, Thomas Todd, and Gabriel Duvall. They were, for the most part, able, learned men, but they paled in comparison with the Chief Justice, John Marshall.

Justice William Johnson had been appointed by President Thomas Jefferson. Jefferson hoped he would offset the nationalistic tendencies of the Court. Johnson has been described as "a loose cannon" who seemed to attract controversy. After he had served on the bench a short while, it appeared that his decisions would be the opposite of what Jefferson wanted. The attorney general of the United States remarked to Jefferson that Johnson "had been infected with leprosy of the Bench."[3]

Supreme Court Justice William Johnson was appointed by President Thomas Jefferson. After he had served on the bench for a short while, however, it appeared that his decisions would be the opposite of what Jefferson had hoped for.

Justice Joseph Story was a brilliant and prolific writer on the law. He had written the important decision in *Martin* v. *Hunter's Lessee* several years before. While he was a member of the Supreme Court, he was also a professor at Harvard Law School. He was appointed to the Court after three other men had declined the job.

Justice Bushrod Washington was George Washington's favorite nephew and eventually inherited his uncle's home, Mount Vernon. He also was in charge of George Washington's public and private papers, which he loaned to John Marshall. Marshall used them to write a biography of George Washington.[4] Bushrod Washington did not write any important opinions. He tended to go along with Justices Marshall and Story. One member of the Court at that time said that Washington's views were so similar to those of Marshall that they "are commonly estimated as a single judge."[5]

Justice Thomas Todd was another disappointment to President Jefferson. Jefferson hoped that he would be a states' rights supporter against the Court's increasing nationalism. He, too, usually followed the lead of Chief Justice Marshall, however. Todd was frequently absent from the Court. These absences were due to illness in his family and the hardships of traveling the long distance to Washington, on poor roads, from his home in Kentucky.

Justice Gabriel Duvall has been described as "one of the least important Justices ever to serve on the United States Supreme Court."[6] During his last ten years on the Court, including the time that *Gibbons* v. *Ogden* was heard, Justice Duvall was ill and deaf.

It was John Marshall who was the star of this Court. He wrote the majority of the opinions "with his colleagues in agreement" that gave increased power to the federal government and the Supreme Court.[7] Through gentle persuasion, he usually was able to get the other Justices to agree with him. This was especially true

Supreme Court Justice Bushrod Washington (shown here) was George Washington's nephew. Bushrod Washington's opinions as a member of the Court tended to go along with those of Justices Marshall and Story.

President Thomas Jefferson (shown here) had hoped that Justice Thomas Todd would support states' rights, but Todd generally followed the nationalistic lead of Chief Justice Marshall.

when the Court reached the decision in *Gibbons* v. *Ogden.*

Unanimous Decision

Marshall still had not completely recovered when the Court announced the unanimous decision. Speaking in a weak voice, he declared that the New York steamboat monopoly grant to Aaron Ogden was unconstitutional. Thomas Gibbons held a license to operate steamboats issued by the national government under the Federal Coasting Act of 1793. In this situation, where state and federal statutes were in conflict, the federal laws prevailed. Just as in previous decisions, such as *Fletcher* v. *Peck* and *McCulloch* v. *Maryland,* Marshall decided strongly in favor of the power of the national government over the states. The power of the Supreme Court to declare state laws unconstitutional was upheld. In this case, it was the question of state laws relating to interstate commerce.

He based his decision on the Commerce Clause of the Constitution, article I, section 8. It gives Congress the power "to regulate Commerce . . . among the several States." His decision gave a broad interpretation to the meaning of commerce.

He began by saying that the words in the Constitution must be understood in their "natural sense." Therefore, commerce among the states must be understood to include navigation on lakes, rivers, streams, and oceans: "The subject to be regulated is commerce. . . . Commerce undoubtedly is traffic."[8] He added that this was a definition everyone understood:

> All America understands, and has uniformly understood, the word "commerce" to comprehend navigation. . . . The power over commerce, including navigation, was one of the primary objects for which the people . . . adopted their government, and must have been contemplated in forming it.[9]

His next point was that commerce, as defined in the Constitution, applies to two areas: commerce with foreign nations and commerce "among the several states." The key phrase was "among the several states," which he said meant that the states were "intermingled" with each other. Therefore, "commerce among the states cannot stop at the external boundary line of each state, but may be introduced into the interior."[10]

Marshall rejected the definition of commerce that meant only the exchange of goods across state lines. Rather, he said, commerce included navigation on waterways to transport passengers. Steamboats carrying passengers from one state to another were therefore part of interstate commerce.

Marshall then demolished the concurrent powers argument that Aaron Ogden's attorneys had proposed.

He said that in the area of interstate commerce the power of Congress was supreme:

> This power, like all others vested in Congress, is complete in itself, may be exercised to its utmost extent, and acknowledges no limitations, other than are prescribed in the constitution. . . . The power over commerce with foreign nations, and among the several states, is vested in Congress as absolutely as it would be in a single government. . . .[11]

He added that: "When a State proceeds to regulate commerce . . . among the several states it is exercising the very power that is granted to Congress, and is doing the very thing that Congress is authorized to do."[12]

Marshall also said that the states still had a role in commerce, however. He emphasized that only the states could regulate the commerce that was entirely within their borders. He also said states had the police power to regulate the health and safety of their citizens. In saying this, he left the door open for the states to claim those rights. In future cases, they would do just that, and frequently they would be upheld by the Court.

The Court had unanimously agreed on the decision, 6–0. There were no dissenting opinions.

A Concurring Opinion

Justice William Johnson, however, read a concurring opinion (an opinion agreeing with the majority opinion) that was an even stronger statement of nationalism than that of Marshall. Never mind that President Jefferson had appointed him to the Court to oppose Marshall's nationalism.

Johnson said the New York monopoly was unconstitutional because only Congress had the power over interstate commerce. He saw no need to use the Federal Coasting Act to strike down a New York law, because the law would have been unconstitutional even if Thomas Gibbons did not hold a federal license.

It was obvious that John Marshall agreed to a great extent with Daniel Webster's argument that a federal statute took precedence over a state law. Marshall and Webster were both nationalists and thought alike on most issues of federal-state relations. Webster himself took credit for the Chief Justice's opinion in *Gibbons*. Several years after the decision was announced he said:

> The opinion of the Court, as rendered by the Chief Justice, was little else than a recital of my argument. The Chief Justice told me that he had little to do but to repeat that argument, as that covered the whole ground.[13]

A few weeks later, when the 1824 Supreme Court term was finished, John Marshall went home to Virginia by steamboat. He had never traveled by steamboat before, and the *Gibbons* case had whetted his appetite for this new way to travel. One of his biographers has written:

> Having broken the steamboat monopoly, . . . Marshall wanted to experience the marvel of moving upstream against a strong current. . . . At the age of sixty-nine, and not fully recovered from a serious injury, the Chief Justice was as excited as a child at the opportunity to return home by steamboat.[14]

7

The Impact of the Gibbons Decision

A few days after the news of the *Gibbons* decision reached New York City, the *United States*, a steamboat owned by some men from Connecticut, sailed into New York Harbor. It had been seventeen years since the *Clermont* had made its first successful trip. Streamers flew from the boat's mast. The large group of passengers cheered as a cannon on board fired a triumphant salute. On the wharf, a crowd of spectators also cheered enthusiastically. Within a few weeks, two boats were named *John Marshall* in honor of the Chief Justice. Soon the steamboat company that had been owned by the Fulton-Livingston interests went out of business and was replaced by various companies under new ownership.

John Marshall had finally issued a popular opinion. Why was public reaction to Gibbons so favorable when it had been so unfavorable to his other nationalistic opinions? The reason was that this decision directly affected so many ordinary people, such as Thomas Gibbons, who wanted to get into the steamboat business. Now the hated monopoly had been struck down, and they could do so.

Newspapers in the North praised the decision and the Chief Justice who wrote it. A few days after the decision was announced a reporter for a New York newspaper wrote: "This opinion . . . presents one of the most powerful efforts of the human mind that has ever been displayed from the bench of any Court. . . . The steamboat grant is at an end."[1] A newspaper in Connecticut called on everyone to consent to a decision that would free the entire nation from monopolies. This reaction could be expected, of course, from one of the states that had fought the Fulton-Livingston monopoly. Other newspapers described the opinion and the Chief Justice as "profound," "masterful," and "farsighted."

Opposition to the Decision

Not everyone was delighted about the *Gibbons* decision, however. Southerners worried that legitimizing the power of Congress over interstate commerce would be a death blow for buying and selling slaves. One vocal southern representative in Congress, a strong states' rights supporter, complained that the opinion went much further than necessary simply to uphold the right of boats to enter New York waters. In a letter to a friend he wrote that "It is the fashion to praise the Chief Justice's opinion. . . . But you know that I am not a fashionable man. I think it is unworthy of him." Later, to another friend, he remarked: "I am done with the Supreme Court."[2]

One of the angriest opponents of the *Gibbons* decision was former president Thomas Jefferson. Now eighty-two years old, Jefferson had attacked all of the Marshall Court's decisions promoting nationalism as harmful to agricultural interests and dangerous to the country. In a letter written two months after the decision, and a year before he died, Jefferson said:

> I see . . . with the deepest affliction, the rapid strides with which the Federal branch of our Government is advancing towards the usurpation of all the rights reserved to the States, and the consolidation in itself of all powers, foreign and domestic. . . . Take together . . . it is but too evident that the three ruling branches [of government] are in combination to strip their colleagues, the State authorities, of the power reserved by them.[3]

James Kent, the judge who ruled in favor of the steamboat monopoly in the New York courts, downplayed the importance of the decision. He pointed out that his ruling had been reversed only on the interpretation of the federal coasting law. He once more emphasized his belief that this law was not a regulation of commerce.

One of the immediate results of the *Gibbons* decision was that the steamboat industry grew rapidly, and steamboat traffic between the states increased. A year after the decision, *Miles Register*, which kept records of such things, reported that the number of steamboats sailing from New York ports had increased from six to forty-three.

This growth of the steamboat industry affected the economy of the country, especially in the Northeast. Some historians say that New York City began to grow as the country's most important commercial center because steamboats could freely transport passengers and merchandise between states.[4] Industries in New England were able to hire steamboats to bring them coal.

Over the years historians have generally praised John Marshall's decision in *Gibbons* v. *Ogden*. One of Marshall's biographers, Albert Beveridge, wrote that this decision "has done more to knit the American people into an indivisible Nation than any other force in our history, excepting only war."[5] Other writers have praised Marshall as a statesman who struck down not only monopolies but also a localism that was out of touch with the reality of a country that was physically expanding across the continent.

Not all legal scholars have thought this way, however. James Bradley Thayer, a nineteenth-century authority on constitutional law, was dissatisfied with the *Gibbons* decision because it gave too much power to Congress and put too many restraints on the states. Another person who criticized the decision was Felix Frankfurter. He was a Supreme Court Justice from 1939 to 1962. Before that he was a Harvard Law School professor. He wrote that Marshall's opinion was "either unconsciously or calculatedly confused" because it was unclear about Congress's exclusive power. He thought that Marshall was interested mainly in preserving the Court's role as an umpire.[6]

The general agreement, however, is that the *Gibbons* decision was one of John Marshall's greatest. It broadly defined the power of Congress over commerce. It made the Commerce Clause of the Constitution the single most important source of regulatory power. It paved the way for tremendous changes in the American economy. And, last but not least, it elevated Marshall to the position of one of the most significant Justices who ever served on the Court. A modern-day legal scholar recently had this to say about the *Gibbons* decision:

Gibbons is the most important commercial case in Supreme Court history. All subsequent nineteenth century Commerce Clause cases [and many twentieth-century ones] were, to a great extent, merely commentary on *Gibbons.*[7]

What John Marshall actually did in his *Gibbons* decision was to take a slight federal involvement with steamboats—the Federal Coasting Act, which licensed boats—and turn it into a federal regulation of interstate commerce. Although the decision broadened the definition of commerce, it still left room for the states to act. According to Marshall's opinion, states could regulate commerce relating to "those internal concerns which . . . are completely within a particular State, which did not affect other States, and which it is not necessary to interfere, for the purpose of executing some of the general powers of the government."[8] Although he did not say so in his opinion, Marshall implied that future cases and courts could settle the issue. So, even though the nationalists cheered and the states' rights supporters condemned the decision, the states still had room to act.

States' rights supporters could relax when they read the Supreme Court decisions in the twenty-five years after *Gibbons.* Even John Marshall acted cautiously, and Congress did not take advantage of the opportunity to exercise its powers relating to interstate commerce. Most cases that reached the Court concerned the question of a state's power to regulate commerce when federal control was unclear.

The first Commerce Clause case the Supreme Court heard after the *Gibbons* decision was in 1837.[9] In an opinion written by John Marshall, the Court ruled that a Maryland statute was unconstitutional because it placed a tax on foreign imports, which was a federal concern. One of the attorneys for the importer who sued the state was William Wirt, who thirteen years before had represented Thomas Gibbons. Then, two years later, the Court decided a case in favor of a state. This case was about a dam that had been built across a stream and was obstructing someone's view. The Court, speaking through Chief Justice John Marshall, ruled that regulating the dam was within the state's police power to regulate the health and safety of its citizens.

This was Marshall's last opinion on a Commerce Clause case. He died in 1835 and was succeeded as Chief Justice by Roger Taney.

Chief Justice Roger Taney

Chief Justice Taney is best known for writing one of the most notorious opinions in Supreme Court history, *Dred Scott* v. *Sandford* in 1857. It is known as the *Dred Scott* case. The Court ruled that African Americans were not citizens of the United States and that Congress had

Dred Scott was a slave who was denied his freedom as a result of the Supreme Court's *Dred Scott* v. *Sandford* decision in 1957.

no power to exclude slavery from any part of the country. Despite this one horrendous lapse, Taney has been ranked by historians as one of the "great" Justices, along with John Marshall and several others, because of his other opinions. Like Marshall, Taney was devoted to the Union, but he also strongly believed in states' rights.

Chief Justice Taney did not have to wait long before a case about the Commerce Clause came before the Court. In 1837 the Court ruled that New York could use its police power to regulate immigrants who lived within its border—in this instance, to remove undesirable aliens. Justice Phillip Barbour wrote the opinion, but Taney concurred. Barbour said that the state had

Roger Brooke Taney is best known for writing the ill-fated decision in the *Dred Scott* case, one of the most notorious opinions in Supreme Court history.

the right to protect itself from nonresidents who might become a burden on society. He suggested that the decision in *Gibbons* did not apply in this case because interstate commerce concerned only merchandise, not people. Justice Joseph Story wrote a dissenting opinion, pointing out that New York's actions did indeed interfere with interstate commerce.

Daniel Webster appeared before the Court again in 1841 to argue that a restriction on slave trade by the state of Mississippi was unconstitutional because it dealt with interstate commerce.[10] This was Webster's first appearance before the Court in a commerce case since *Gibbons*. He told the Justices that "the Constitution confers on Congress the right to regulate commerce . . . In the case of *Gibbons* v. *Ogden* it was decided, that it extends to all commerce between state. . . . Nothing which is affected by commerce, can be affected by state law."[11] Webster was implying that he hoped the Court would adopt a new rule that limited state power even if Congress had not acted on the subject. The Justices engaged in a lively debate about the commerce power. Then they voted by a narrow margin to uphold the Mississippi law.

The concurrent powers idea that Aaron Ogden's attorneys had argued began to creep into decisions a few years later. The Court, in 1847, upheld the laws of several New England states that required anyone who sold even a small amount of liquor to purchase a license. Six Justices who voted with the majority nevertheless each issued separate opinions. Some said that the state statutes were legitimate police powers of the state, and some said that these regulations fell under the concurrent powers of the states and national government. Chief Justice Taney wrote that a state could regulate interstate commerce until Congress passed a law on the subject. He added that *Gibbons* had not decided that the national government had exclusive power over interstate commerce:

> It appears to me to be very clear that the mere grant of power to the central government cannot, upon any just principles of construction, be construed to be an absolute prohibition to the exercise of any power over the same subject by the States.[12]

Cooley v. *Board of Wardens*

The decision in which the idea of concurrent powers was a key point was *Cooley* v. *Board of Wardens of the Port of Philadelphia* in 1852.[13] This case also had to do with boats. In 1803, Pennsylvania had enacted a requirement that any boat sailing into the state's harbors had to pay a fee unless the boat's owner hired local pilots or helmsmen. This fee was used to care for pilots' widows and orphans. The law was challenged on the grounds that it was a regulation of interstate commerce and therefore not subject to the jurisdiction of state lawmakers. The issue revolved around two questions: Did the constitutional grant of commerce power to Congress automatically prohibit state regulation of commerce? Or could states regulate commerce as long as these regulations did not actually conflict with laws passed by Congress?

This opinion was written by Justice Benjamin Curtis. He was a friend of that great nationalist, Daniel Webster, who had recommended his appointment to the Court. The *Cooley* decision was a compromise between national powers and states' rights. Justice Curtis said that the commerce power that was granted to Congress did not always exclude the states. Curtis's opinion emphasized that the subject being regulated was the important issue. He pointed out that some subjects were national in scope and some were local; in other words, the national government and the states had concurrent power. This became known as the Cooley Doctrine. In this particular case, the regulation of fees was a local matter. According to a modern historian, this decision, along with *Gibbons*, "ranks as one of the most important commerce clause cases of the nineteenth century."[14]

Two Justices filed dissenting opinions. To support

their disagreement, they relied on John Marshall's main point about the supremacy of the national government in interstate commerce.

Surprisingly, Congress did not immediately take advantage of the go-ahead to act in the area of commerce. The country went through another growth spurt after the Civil War. Businesses grew and consolidated, and the railroads spread out across the country. Congress had several opportunities to pass legislation dealing with corporation growth, poor working conditions, and the beginning of a population move from farms to cities, but the national government was probably too busy dealing with the problems arising from slavery and the Civil War.

However, during the last two decades of the nineteenth century, Congress began to act. In 1887 lawmakers passed a statute that established the Interstate Commerce Commission to regulate railroad rates. Other similar laws soon followed that regulated working conditions and big business.

Soon some of the same issues in *Gibbons* reached the Supreme Court, but in a slightly different form. Whether the Justices sided with the states or the national government, they based their decisions on *Gibbons*.

For example, in the *Granger* case, the Court upheld

a state's regulation of railroad rates. Chief Justice Morrison Waite said these regulations did not infringe on interstate commerce. However, just nine years later, in a case called *Wabash Railway* v. *Illinois,* in an opinion by Justice Samuel Miller, the Court ruled that some similar state regulations were illegal because they dealt with interstate commerce. He stated that the state of Illinois was regulating interstate traffic. He did not call for national regulation, which he could have done, but instead indicated that he disliked all state restraints on the freedom of commerce.

The Justices could not seem to make up their minds about what were legitimate state regulations and what were legitimate national regulations in cases that they heard in the early twentieth century. One of the most famous cases of that era involving the Commerce Clause was *Swift* v. *United States* in 1905.[15] This case dealt with antitrust action against the Beef Trust, which had cornered the cattle industry, in effect creating a monopoly. Speaking for the Court, Justice Oliver Wendell Holmes established the "stream of commerce" doctrine. This meant that Congress could regulate interstate commerce that included a series of acts, from the shipping to the sale of cattle, even though there were temporary interruptions in this "stream" or flow.

In a decision two years before, in 1903, the Justices

Supreme Court Justice Oliver Wendell Holmes established the stream of commerce doctrine in the *Swift* v. *United States* decision of 1905.

had ruled that Congress could use its commerce power as a police power to outlaw the sale and shipment of lottery tickets between states. A few years later, they ruled that Congress did not have the power to outlaw certain types of labor union contracts because labor relations were not part of interstate commerce. In another case, the Justices ruled that Congress can regulate railroad rates if this regulation is necessary to ensure effective regulation of interstate rates. Shortly after, in a famous case called *Hammer* v. *Dagenhart*, in 1918, the Justices ruled that Congress could not use its commerce power as a police power to limit the number of hours that children could work, because this would be an unconstitutional attempt to regulate manufacturing, which was not commerce.[16]

The real action in the Supreme Court came during the Great Depression of the 1930s. The Depression began after the stock market crashed in 1929. This was a period of severe economic problems. More than 15 million people were out of work. People lost their homes and farms because they did not have money to pay the mortgages. Millions of people lost their savings, and thousands of banks went bankrupt. Many companies went out of business.

In 1932 the American voters elected Franklin Roosevelt, a Democrat, as president. He promised the

American people a "New Deal" to end the Depression and make the country economically healthy again. The voters also elected a Democratic Congress, which supported the president's New Deal programs. These programs included the National Industrial Recovery Act (NIRA) to help businesses, the Agricultural Adjustment Act (AAA) to help farmers, an act establishing the Securities and Exchange Commission (SEC) to reform the stock market, and the Federal Emergency Relief Act. Both the NIRA and the AAA were declared unconstitutional by the Supreme Court, as we shall see. Economic conditions did not really improve until 1940, when the United States became involved in World War II. Military and industrial spending increased to help the war effort, which created a demand for workers and goods.

Schecter Poultry Corp. v. United States

At first, the Court overturned much of the New Deal legislation that President Franklin Delano Roosevelt had proposed and Congress had passed. One of the first cases where the Court overturned a New Deal economic recovery measure was *Schecter Poultry Corp. v. United States* in 1935.[17] The Court declared that the National Industrial Recovery Act was unconstitutional. The opinion was written by Chief Justice Charles Evans

Hughes. Hughes referred again to the stream of commerce doctrine from the *Swift* case of 1905. He wrote that this doctrine did not allow Congress to regulate a company that received products from another state but sold them locally. Needless to say, the president and the Democrats in Congress who helped him with his New Deal program were angry at the Court. President Roosevelt was as hostile toward the Supreme Court as President Thomas Jefferson had been during John Marshall's time almost a hundred years before.

Butler v. United States

Then, another decision in 1936 angered Roosevelt even more. In *Butler* v. *United States* the Court, in an opinion by Justice Owen Roberts, ruled that the Agricultural Adjustment Act was unconstitutional.[18] The Court said that Congress had no authority to regulate agricultural production by requiring a tax on processors of food in order to pay benefits to farmers who reduced production of certain crops. Butler, a processor, had refused to pay the tax. Roberts's opinion included a long explanation of his belief that the Court had only a limited role in deciding constitutional questions. One constitutional historian called Roberts's opinion "monumentally inept."[19] Several Justices wrote

American voters elected Franklin Delano Roosevelt as president in 1932. He promised the American people a plan called the New Deal as a means to end the economic depression in the country.

dissenting opinions. Justice Benjamin Cardozo called Roberts's ruling "a tortured construction of the Constitution." And Justice Harlan F. Stone criticized his fellow Justices: "Courts are not the only agency of government that must be assumed to have capacity to govern. . . . The only check upon our own exercise of power is our own self-restraint."[20]

The president agreed with the dissenters that the Supreme Court had gone too far. In contrast to President Thomas Jefferson in the early nineteenth century, who wrote angry letters, President Roosevelt decided to act. In early 1937, the president sent to Congress a bill to change the makeup of the federal courts. Opponents immediately called this the "court-packing bill." The bill would have allowed a president to appoint one Supreme Court Justice for every Justice who was over age seventy, up to a total of six. Obviously Roosevelt wanted to appoint Justices who would agree with his New Deal legislation. This was not a popular idea, despite many people's unhappiness with recent Court decisions. Republicans, prominent attorneys, southern and moderate northern Democrats, and many newspaper editors harshly criticized the bill. Even many Supreme Court Justices who had supported the president's New Deal legislation denounced this idea.

Something happened a month later, however.

Justice Roberts suddenly switched sides and led the Court to uphold the constitutionality of several pieces of New Deal legislation. This move has been called "the switch in time that saved nine," meaning that the Court "switched" positions and held the number of Justices to nine. For the next decade, the Court relaxed its strict interpretation of what constituted interstate commerce and what was permissible legislation for Congress to enact under the Commerce Clause.

Cases Involving the Commerce Clause

This trend continued throughout the 1960s and even affected civil rights legislation. For example, in *Heart of Atlanta* v. *United States* in 1947, Justice Tom Clark wrote that Congress might use its commerce power to prohibit private persons who operated public accommodations that served an interstate clientele or used goods made in interstate commerce from discriminating on the basis of race.[21]

But the Court favored the states in a 1976 case called *National League of Cities* v. *Usery*.[22] Here Justice William Rehnquist (who today is Chief Justice) wrote that Congress had exceeded its commerce power when it established wage and hour standards for state employees because these standards were an unconstitutional infringement of state authority. However, nine years later, the Court reversed this decision. In *Garcia* v. *San Antonio Metropolitan Transit Authority*, the Court ruled that Congress had the authority to set federal minimum wage and hour standards for state employees because the Constitution provided sufficient safeguards to protect the states' interests even when Congress acted.[23]

In 1995 the Supreme Court decided a case that would have amazed John Marshall. He could not have predicted that the Commerce Clause would someday involve the issue of guns near a public school, but that is exactly what happened. A twelfth-grade student had brought a .35-caliber handgun and five bullets to his high school in Texas. He was convicted under a federal law called the Gun-Free School Zones Act. This law made it a federal offense to "knowingly possess a firearm" in a school zone. Chief Justice William Rehnquist wrote the opinion for the Court in *United States* v. *Lopez*.[24] He wrote that the Gun-Free Act was unconstitutional because it exceeded the authority of Congress "to regulate commerce among the several states." Four other Justices agreed with him. Rehnquist said even though a series of cases over the years broadened the power of Congress under the Commerce Clause, that power "is subject to outer limits." He disagreed with the attorneys for the United States government who said that possession of firearms in a

In 1995 Chief Justice William Rehnquist wrote the opinion for the Supreme Court in *United States* v. *Lopez*, a case that used the Commerce Clause to deal with the issue of guns near a public school.

school zone might affect the functioning of the national economy, especially because the cost of violent crimes is so high that the whole nation suffers. Justice Stephen Breyer, the newest Justice on the Court, disagreed. He wrote in his dissenting opinion that "the statute falls well within the scope of the Commerce Clause as this Court has understood that power over the last half-century."[25] Three other Justices also dissented.

For more than 150 years, the Supreme Court has wrestled with the problem of how much authority Congress has over interstate commerce. From a steamboat owned by a monopoly to a teenager who brought a gun to school, the Court has never really established a definite answer. It has, however, based its decisions on the opinion of John Marshall when he broke up the steamboat monopoly: The source of the power over commerce is in Congress rather than in the states.

Questions for Discussion

1. Pretend that it is the end of the eighteenth century. Choose two members of your class to play the roles of Robert Fulton and Robert Livingston. The rest of the class will be the state lawmakers of New York in 1798. This was the year the lawmakers granted Fulton and Livingston their first steamboat monopoly.

   Fulton and Livingston are presenting to the lawmakers their reasons for wanting a steamboat monopoly. What arguments will they use to convince the lawmakers that they need a monopoly grant in order to run a successful business?

   The lawmakers are not very impressed with this new invention, the steamboat, but they are willing to listen. On what reasons will the lawmakers base their decision to grant a monopoly? Will anyone oppose the idea? What reasons will they give?

2. Many Americans living in the early 1820s were frightened that the new nation would not stay united but would break up into separate states, almost like separate countries, each acting in its own interests and pursuing its own agenda. Many other Americans were hoping that this would happen. What arguments do you think the nationalists had to support their view? What arguments do you think the states' rights supporters had for their view?

3. Imagine that you are Aaron Ogden and you want the public to know it is important for you to continue operating your steamboats under the Fulton-Livingston monopoly. Since neither television nor the Internet exists yet, you have to rely on letters to the editor and speeches at public gatherings. Write letters to two newspaper editors, one in New York and the other in New Jersey, explaining your reasons.

4. Imagine that you are Thomas Gibbons and you want the public to know why it is important to get rid of the Fulton-Livingston monopoly. Write letters to two newspaper editors, one in New York and one in New Jersey.

5. Imagine that you are a member of the Supreme Court when *Gibbons* was heard—either John Marshall, William Johnson, Joseph Story, Bushard Washington, Thomas Todd, or Gabriel Duvall. Every night, when you return to the boardinghouse where you live, you write in your journal about the Court proceedings. Write what you think about the arguments presented by the attorneys for each side. Which attorneys are the most persuasive and why? Do you know how you are going to vote even before you sit down with the other Justices to discuss the decision? Do you think the decision in this case will be important for the future? Explain your answer.

6. Suppose that your state lawmakers are considering a bill that would regulate information coming over the Internet. Could they do this based on the *Gibbons* decision? Explain your answer.

7. Look through your daily newspaper for two weeks. Keep a list of any action that either Congress or the Supreme Court takes relating to interstate commerce. Are there any similarities to the events that led up to *Gibbons*?

8. *Gibbons* ended the steamboat monopoly, but monopolies still exist in some businesses. Can you name some? Look through the business section of your local newspaper and clip any articles dealing with business monopolies. Are modern monopolies very different from the one given to Fulton and Livingston for steamboats? How are they different?

9. In the *Lopez* decision, the Supreme Court ruled that the Gun-Free School Zones Act exceeded the authority of Congress "to regulate commerce among the several states." The Justices who wrote a dissenting opinion said that "the statute falls well within the scope of the Commerce Clause as this Court has understood that power over the last half-century." Do you think that carrying a gun near a school has anything to do with interstate commerce? Explain your answer.

Chapter Notes

Chapter 1. The Journey Begins

1. H. M. Dickinson, *Robert Fulton, Engineer and Artist: His Life and Works* (London: John Lane, 1913), p. 218.

2. Albert J. Beveridge, *The Life of John Marshall: Frontiersman, Soldier, Lawmaker, 1755–1788*, vol. 1 (Boston: Houghton Mifflin Company, 1919), p. 398.

3. Alice Crary Sutcliffe, *Robert Fulton and the "Clermont"* (New York: The Century Company, 1909), p. 204.

4. Bernard Bailyn, David Brion Davis et al., *The Great Republic: A History of the American People*, vol. 1, 2nd ed. (Lexington, Mass.: D. C. Heath & Company, 1981), p. 318.

Chapter 2. America Becomes a Nation

1. Melvin I. Urofsky, *A March of Liberty: A Constitutional History of the United States*, vol. 1 (New York: Alfred A. Knopf, 1988), p. 206.

2. Francis N. Stites, *John Marshall: Defender of the Constitution* (Boston: Little, Brown, and Company, 1981), p. 5.

3. Ibid., p. 3.

4. Kermit L. Hall, ed., *The Oxford Companion to the Supreme Court of the United States* (New York: Oxford University Press, 1992), p. 523.

5. Jean Edward Smith, *John Marshall: Definer of a Nation* (New York: Henry Holt and Company, 1996), p. 63.

6. Hall, p. 523.

7. Smith, p. 122.

8. Charles Warren, *The Supreme Court in United States History: 1789–1835*, vol. 1 (Boston: Little, Brown, & Company, 1922), p. 464.

9. Herbert A. Johnson, *The Chief Justiceship of John Marshall, 1801–1835* (Columbia, S.C.: University of South Carolina Press, 1997), p. 1.

10. 1 Cranch (5 U.S.) 137 (1803).

11. 6 Cranch (10 U.S.) 87 (1810).

12. *Fairfax's Devisee* v. *Hunter's Lessee* 7 Cranch (11 U.S.) 603 (1813).

13. 1 Wheat. (14 U.S.) 304 (1816).

14. Smith, p. 127.

15. Hall, p. 529.

16. 4 Wheat. (17 U.S.) 518 (1819).

17. 4 Wheat. (17 U.S.) 316 (1819).

18. Ibid., p. 408.

Chapter 3. The Road to the Supreme Court

1. *Livingston* v. *Van Ingen*, 9 Johns. 507 (New York, 1812).

2. George Dangerfield, "The Steamboat Case," in *Quarrels That Have Shaped the Constitution*, ed. John A. Garraty, rev. ed. (New York: Harper & Row, 1987), p. 60.

3. Maurice G. Baxter, *The Steamboat Monopoly: Gibbons v. Ogden, 1824* (New York: Alfred A. Knopf, 1972), p. 31.

4. *Livingston* v. *Van Ingen*, 9 Johns. 507 (New York, 1812).

5. 17 Johns. 488 (New York, 1820).

6. Kermit L. Hall, ed., *The Oxford Companion to the Supreme Court of the United States* (New York: Oxford University Press, 1992), p. 39.

Chapter 4. The Case for Thomas Gibbons

1. Charles Warren, *The Supreme Court in the United States History: 1789–1835*, vol. 1 (Boston: Little, Brown, & Company, 1922), p. 461.

2. Maurice G. Baxter, *The Steamboat Monopoly: Gibbons v. Ogden, 1824* (New York: Alfred A. Knopf, 1972), p. 39.

3. Jean Edward Smith, *John Marshall: Definer of a Nation* (New York: Henry Holt and Co., 1996), p. 475.

4. *Livingston* v. *Van Ingen*, 9 Johns. 507 (New York, 1812).

5. Phillip Kurland and Gerhard Casper, *Landmark Briefs and Arguments of the Supreme Court of the United States* (Arlington, Va.: University Publications of America, 1978), p. 359.

6. Ibid., p. 363.

7. Ibid., p. 367.

8. Ibid.

9. Smith, p. 475.

Chapter 5. The Case for Aaron Ogden

1. Albert Beveridge, *The Life of John Marshall: The Building of the Nation, 1815–1835*, vol. 4 (Boston: Houghton Mifflin Company, 1919), pp. 423–424.

2. Ibid., p. 424.

3. Maurice G. Baxter, *The Steamboat Monopoly: Gibbons v. Ogden, 1824* (New York: Alfred A. Knopf, 1972), p. 43.

4. Jean Edward Smith, *John Marshall: Definer of a Nation* (New York: Henry Holt and Company, 1996), pp. 465–476.

5. Phillip Kurland and Gerhard Casper, *Landmark Briefs and Arguments of the Supreme Court of the United States* (Arlington, Va.: University Publications of America, 1989), p. 359.

6. Ibid.

7. Baxter, p. 39.

8. G. Edward White, *The Marshall Court and Cultural Change, 1815–35* (New York: Macmillan Publishing Co., 1988), p. 212.

Chapter 6. The Decision

1. 9 Wheat. (22 U.S.) 1 (1824).

2. Jean Edward Smith, *John Marshall: Definer of a Nation* (New York: Henry Holt and Company, 1996), p. 476.

3. Kermit L. Hall, ed., *The Oxford Companion to the Supreme Court of the United States* (New York: Oxford University Press, 1991), p. 449.

4. Ibid., p. 917.

5. Ibid.

6. Ibid., p. 240.

7. Smith, p. 477.

8. Joan Biskupic and Elder Witt, *The Supreme Court and the Powers of the American Government* (Washington, D.C.: Congressional Quarterly, Inc., 1997), p. 69.

9. Ibid.

10. Ibid.

11. Ibid.

12. Ibid., p. 40.

13. Charles Warren, *The Supreme Court in the United States History: 1789–1835*, vol. 2 (Boston: Little, Brown, & Company, 1922), pp. 70–71.

14. Smith, p. 481.

Chapter 7. The Impact of the Gibbons Decision

1. Charles Warren, *The Supreme Court in the United States History: 1789–1835*, vol. 2 (Boston: Little, Brown, & Company, 1922), p. 73.

2. Maurice G. Baxter, *The Steamboat Monopoly: Gibbons v. Ogden, 1824* (New York: Alfred A. Knopf, 1972), p. 70.

3. Warren, p. 80.

4. Ibid., p. 76.

5. Albert J. Beveridge, *The Life of John Marshall: The Building of the Nation, 1815–1835*, vol. 4 (Boston: Houghton Mifflin Company, 1919), p. 430.

6. Baxter, p. 62.

7. Kermit L. Hall, William M. Wiececk, and Paul Finkelman, *American Legal History: Cases and Materials* (New York: Oxford University Press, 1991), p. 125.

8. Joan Biskupic and Elder Witt, *The Supreme Court and the Powers of the American Government* (Washington, D.C.: Congressional Quarterly, Inc., 1997), p. 69.

9. *Brown* v. *Maryland*, 12 Wheat. (25 U.S.) 419 (1827).

10. *Groves* v. *Slaughter*, 15 Pet. (40 U.S.) 449 (1841).

11. Baxter, pp. 95–96.

12. *"License Cases,"* 5 Howard (46 U.S.) 504 (1847).

13. 12 How. (53 U.S.) 299 (1852).

14. Hall et al., p. 197.

15. 196 U.S. 375 (1905).

16. 247 U.S. 251 (1918).

17. 295 U.S. 495 (1935).

18. 297 U.S. 1 (1936).

19. Leonard Levy, quoted in Kermit L. Hall, *The Oxford Companion to the Supreme Court of the United States* (New York: Oxford University Press, 1992), p. 111.

20. Hall et al., p. 111.

21. 379 U.S. 241 (1964).

22. 426 U.S. 833 (1976).

23. 469 U.S. 528 (1985).

24. 514 U.S. 549 (1995).

25. Duane Lockart and Walter Murphy, *Basic Cases in Constitutional Law*, 3rd ed. (Washington, D.C.: Congressional Quarterly Press, 1992), p. 116.

Glossary

abstain—Not participate.

appeal—Take a case from a lower to a higher court for a new hearing.

brief—A written argument presented by the attorneys in a lawsuit.

chamber—The room where court sessions are held.

charter—To establish an institution with certain privileges.

Chief Justice—The senior judge of the Supreme Court.

Commerce Clause—Article I, section 8 of the United States Constitution, which gives Congress the power to regulate business matters between the states.

concurrent powers—The principle of government that says that both Congress and the individual states have authority to pass laws in the same area.

concurring opinion—An opinion written by a Justice who agrees with the decision of the court but disagrees with the reason for the decision.

contract—An enforceable agreement between two bodies or entities.

Contract Clause—Article I, section 10 of the United States Constitution, which prohibits states from passing laws that would damage a contract.

court—The judge or judges who listen to arguments in a lawsuit.

court of chancery—A court that administers justice according to rules of equity or fairness rather than following the strict rules of law.

dissenting opinion—An opinion written by a Justice who disagrees with the majority decision of the court.

docket—A list of cases to be considered by a court.

injunction—An order from a court to prohibit someone from doing a specific act.

interstate commerce—Business activities between states.

judicial review—The process in which the courts can review acts of the executive and legislative bodies.

Justices—The members who sit on the Supreme Court.

litigant—The party to a lawsuit.

monopoly—An exclusive privilege to participate in an activity.

opinion—A written explanation of a court's decision.

repeal—To withdraw a law.

revoke—To take away.

states' rights—The belief that the individual states have more authority than the national government.

statute—A law passed by a legislative body.

turnpikes—Rough roads that connected towns in the eighteenth and nineteenth centuries.

Further Reading

Brandt, Clare. *An American Aristocracy: The Livingstons.* New York: Doubleday & Company, Inc., 1986.

Feinberg, Barbara Silberdick. *John Marshall: The Great Chief Justice.* Springfield, N.J.: Enslow Publishers, Inc., 1995.

Garraty, John A. *Quarrels That Have Shaped the Constitution.* New York: Harper & Row, 1987.

Hall, Kermit L. *The Magic Mirror: Law in American History.* New York: Oxford University Press, 1989.

———. *The Oxford Companion to the Supreme Court of the United States.* New York: Oxford University Press, 1991.

Horwitz, Morton J. *The Transformation of American Law, 1780–1960: The Crisis of Legal Orthodoxy.* New York: Oxford University Press, 1992.

Johnson, Herbert A. *The Chief Justiceship of John Marshall, 1801–1835.* Columbia, S.C.: University of South Carolina Press, 1997.

Kurland, Philip, and Gerhard Casper. *Landmark Briefs and Arguments of the Supreme Court of the United States.* Vol. 1. Arlington, Va.: University Publications of America, 1978.

Newmyer, R. Kent. *Supreme Court Justice Joseph Story: Statesman of the Old Republic.* Chapel Hill, N.C.: University of North Carolina Press, 1985.

Philip, Cynthia. *Robert Fulton: A Biography.* New York: Franklin Watts, 1985.

Remini, Robert V. *Daniel Webster: The Man and His Time.* New York: W. W. Norton & Company, 1997.

Shewmaker, Kenneth E., ed. *Daniel Webster: "The Completest Man."* Hanover, N.H., and London: Dartmouth College University Press of New England, 1990.

Smith, Jean Edward. *John Marshall: Definer of a Nation.* New York: Henry Holt and Company, 1996.

Stites, Francis N. *John Marshall: Defender of the Constitution.* Boston: Little, Brown and Company, 1981.

Urofsky, Melvin I. *A March of Liberty: A Constitutional History of the United States,* vol. 1: to 1877. New York: Alfred A. Knopf, 1988.

White, G. Edward. *The Marshall Court and Cultural Change, 1815–1835.* New York: Macmillan Publishing Company, 1988.

Internet Addresses:

Northwestern University Law School:
<http://oyez.nwu.edu/cases/cases.cgi>

Interstate Commerce:
<http://lcweb.loc.gov/lexico/liv/i/Interstate_commerce.html>

Steamboats:
<http://www.steamboats.com>

Index